THE
INSULATED
TANK
REVOLUTION

Boost Efficiency, Streamline Processes, and Maximize Results in Your Projects Execution with Innovative Sustainable Water Storage Solutions.

THE
INSULATED TANK REVOLUTION

Boost Efficiency, Streamline Processes, and Maximize Results in Your Projects Execution with Innovative Sustainable Water Storage Solutions.

For MES and CPWD GEs, EEs,CEs, and CWEs

V.K. AGGARWAL

Worldwide Published by

Pendown Press

PENDOWN PRESS LLP
An ISO 9001 & ISO 14001 Certified Co.,
Regd. Office: 3767A, Kanhaiya Nagar,
Tri Nagar, Delhi-110035
Ph.: 8130886000, 9650072927, 8595249536
E-mail: info@pendownpress.com
Branch Office: 1A/2A, 20, Hari Sadan, Ansari Road,
Daryaganj, New Delhi-110002
Ph.: 011-45794768
Website: PendownPress.com

First Edition: 2023
Price: ₹499/-
ISBN: 978-93-5554-653-1

Layout and Cover Designed by Pendown Graphics Team
Printed and Bound in India by Thomson Press India Ltd.

Contents

Chapter 1

The Beginning

The reason behind my endeavor to write this book is rooted in my desire to effectively communicate my message to a wide range of professionals involved in infrastructure project execution, including Garrison Engineers, Engineers in Chief, Executive Engineers, Commander Works Engineers, and others. After extensive research on various communication media, I have concluded that a book is the most potent and expedient method to disseminate my ideas. A book has the remarkable ability to transcend geographical boundaries and reach far-flung places, carrying my message to readers even in my absence. Today, I stand before you with the purpose of presenting something significant, and this book serves as the medium through which I aim to accomplish that goal.

Through my observations, I have noticed that many government officials, including Garrison Engineers, Engineers in Chief, and Executive Engineers, encounter challenges or difficulties in their respective roles. This realization has compelled me to write a book specifically targeted towards these professionals. However, it is important to note that while the content of this book is applicable to various industries and departments, such as private builders, rainwater harvesting system installers, fire safety system installers, project owners, poultry farm owners and project management professionals, its primary focus remains on addressing the needs of Garrison Engineers, Engineers in Chief, and Executive Engineers. If you fall into this category, then "The Insulated Tank Revolution" is a book tailored specifically for you. I can humbly assure you that you cannot afford to ignore this book.

1.1 About Me

Apart from being the author of this book (also known as Vinay Garg), I am an unwavering researcher and innovator with over seventeen years of experience in various sectors such as manufacturing, construction, agriculture, poultry farming and rainwater harvesting. Through my dedication and the support of my peers and higher powers, I have developed a unique design in water storage technology that has been recognized and granted a patent by the Intellectual Property India. As of now, no individual or company in India has received a patent for this specific water storage technology.

With my expertise as a polymer scientist, I embarked on the journey of research seventeen years ago. Three years ago, I further solidified my knowledge and credentials by pursuing a Ph.D. degree. Currently, I hold the position of CEO at Himganga Polymers India Pvt Ltd, an acknowledged and authorized organization by MES, CPWD and many prominent govt. departments that specializes in water engineering, water storage solutions, and project execution guidance through the VG-framework (Victory Guaranteed).

Throughout my career, I have successfully delivered numerous projects in collaboration with renowned companies such as L&T, Punj Lloyd, Jindal Groups, Shapoorji, and many others, across seven countries. In recognition of my contribution to providing innovative and modern water storage solutions, I have been honored with an award by MSME of India.

1.2 Our Story

Since our establishment in 1980, we have been dedicated to research and development, as well as manufacturing. Throughout the years, we have proudly served over 1,000 projects spanning seven countries, solidifying our expertise and establishing a global presence.

Our unwavering dedication and commitment to excellence has not gone unnoticed. We have been honored and recognized by numerous central and state government agencies, acknowledging our exceptional contributions to the industry. This recognition highlights our commitment to delivering high-quality solutions and our adherence to industry standards.

One of our notable achievements included being awarded by the prestigious The Economic Journal for our innovative work in the manufacturing and construction industry. This recognition underscores our commitment to pushing boundaries and introducing groundbreaking solutions that propel progress within the sector.

Furthermore, we have achieved a significant milestone through the innovation of a unique design that has received acceptance and a patent from the Government of India. This recognition showcases our ability to think outside the box and develop solutions that meet the specific needs of our clients and the industry as a whole.

We take great pride in being honored by the MSME (Micro, Small, and Medium Enterprises) of India for our dedication to providing innovative and modern water storage solutions. This recognition reinforces our commitment to sustainability, efficiency, and meeting the evolving demands of the market.

As we continue our journey, we remain steadfast in our pursuit of excellence, innovation, and utmost customer satisfaction. We are driven by the belief that our work makes a positive impact on the industry, the communities we serve, and the environment as a whole.

1.3 Our Journey

1980: Unregistered Trading Firm

In 1980, we embarked on our journey as an unregistered trading firm, laying the foundation for our future endeavors in the industry.

2000: Registered Manufacturing Company

In the year 2000, we established ourselves as a registered manufacturing company enabling us to expand our operations and serve a wider customer base.

Enlisting in Government Departments

During this time, we actively pursued partnerships with various government departments such as CPWD (Central Public Works Department) and MES (Military Engineering Services). Our goal was to provide our high-quality products and services to government projects, thereby establishing a strong presence in the public sector.

2010: Becoming a Trusted Company

By 2010, we had earned the trust and confidence of our clients, both in the government and private sectors. This trust was a result of our unwavering commitment to delivering reliable and top-notch solutions.

Expanding Reach and Establishing R&D Department

During this period, we expanded our reach and successfully collaborated with a wide range of government departments and private companies. Moreover, we established an in-house Research and Development (R&D) department, empowering us to innovate and develop cutting-edge solutions that cater to the evolving needs of the industry.

2015: An Important Milestone - Innovative Water Storage Solution

In 2015, we achieved a significant milestone in our journey. We successfully innovated a new technology for water storage solutions, revolutionizing the industry with our groundbreaking approach.

2019: Acceptance of Patent by Intellectual Property India

Our unwavering commitment to innovation and intellectual property protection led to a significant accomplishment in 2019. One of our patents was accepted by the Intellectual Property India, recognizing the uniqueness and value of our invention.

Throughout our journey, we have worked tirelessly to establish ourselves as a trusted and reliable company. We take pride in our extensive coverage of government departments and private companies, ensuring our products and services reach a wide range of customers.

Looking ahead, we will continue to drive innovation, deliver exceptional solutions, and further solidify our reputation as a leading player in the industry.

Our Journey

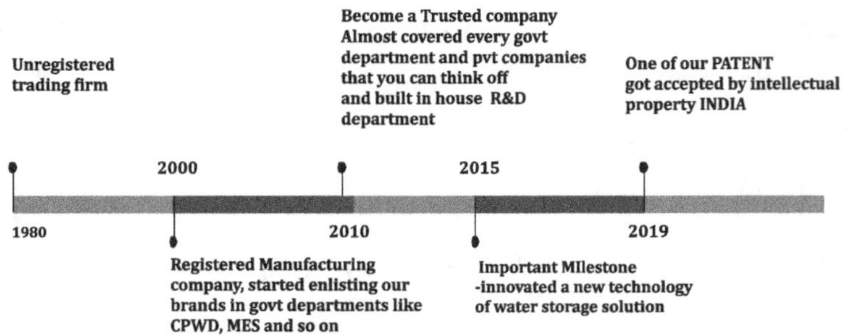

1.4 How we solved the problems: Testimonials

First, I was hesitant about whom to include. Then, I recalled an interesting story about a renowned and prestigious company, let's refer to it as "Earth Builders LTD" (actual name cannot be revealed due to a NDA with the company). This company operates in the construction field, primarily focusing on government infrastructure projects. The remarkable thing about this company was its visionary nature and the tremendous passion exhibited by its Managing Director. However, there were a few challenges that both the MD and I believe you might be facing as well. One major struggle was the lack of a structured approach or strategy to identify the right product that could effectively meet the required needs. The company relied on ancient ways of procuring the products and executing projects. i.e. there was a meager existence of modern technology and innovative products. As a result, the company incurred significant financial losses each year or even sooner due to the need for frequent product replacements. Furthermore, there was no established structure, system, or mechanism to verify the authenticity of the supplied products. The company had to rely on the papers submitted by vendors, contractors, or subcontractors, only to discover upon investigation that many of these documents were false or fabricated, and often colluded by supervisors or managers . Thus, despite investing in high-cost materials, they failed to meet the company's requirements. Similar cases of duplicity also emerged, where entire products were found to be counterfeited, again due to the collusion between contractors and supervisors.

All in all, it was incurring massive losses to the company. When we audited the purchase data for one year, we were astonished to find that the figure amounted to crores. Fortunately, the MD took the gigantic action to clean up this mess and applied the new framework suggested and hand held by me. Within a few months of implementing the new processes and framework, the company has transformed its situation. They are now not only procuring the right and authentic products but also actively exploring and adopting innovative designs, products, and technologies. As a result, they have started reaping the benefits, including a 10X profit, peace of mind, repeat work, recognition, and awards.

"Mr. VK is an expert with amazing practical experience and knowledge. With his invaluable support, our processes have become smoother, more transparent, and significantly more profitable. His insights and guidance have been invaluable in driving our success. We are immensely grateful to have him on board."

~Naveen Kumar,
Infra Projects Head - L&T

"I am thankful to VK for his wonderful support and expert opinions, which have resulted in saving crores of Rupees for us. His exceptional understanding of the industry and meticulous attention to detail has been instrumental in identifying cost-saving opportunities.

Hats off to you, Vinay!"

~Dharmendra Kaushik,
CEO Structowell Concorp
(Rainwater harvesting, fire safety and water conservation)

"As suppliers of poultry equipment, we have always faced challenges in maintaining water at a specific temperature throughout the day in a hygienic manner. Poultries consume highest water at temperatures up to 27°C, and beyond that, water intake decreases drastically, resulting in slower poultry growth and impacting the profits of poultry farm owners. Despite significant investments and trying various solutions available in the market, we were unable to achieve the desired results until we encountered Vinay. We are immensely grateful to him for his expertise and the solutions he provided. Now, all our clients are delighted to witness the improved growth of their poultry and increased profitability by manifolds."

Sagar Agarwal,

MD - Sagar Poultries

(Poultry Equipment and Water Supply)

These testimonials emphasize Mr. Vinay's expertise and the significant positive impact he has had on the organizations he has collaborated with. By including these testimonials in your book, you will further validate his outstanding contributions and underscore the immense value he brings to the industry.

1.5 Our proud customers

Currently, we proudly serve a wide range of esteemed government departments and organizations. Some of the notable ones include:

1. CPWD (Central Public Works Department)

2. MES (Military Engineering Services)

3. NBCC (National Buildings Construction Corporation)

4. ITBP (Indo-Tibetan Border Police)

5. DRDO (Defence Research and Development Organization)

6. CRPF (Central Reserve Police Force)

7. Indian Air Force

8. ISRO (Indian Space Research Organization)

9. ESIC (Employees' State Insurance Corporation)

10. DMRC (Delhi Metro Rail Corporation)

11. Indian Railways

12. BSF (Border Security Force)

13. Indian Police

14. BHEL (Bharat Heavy Electricals Limited)

15. DDA (Delhi Development Authority)

These are just a few examples, and we have a wide range of clientele spanning various government departments and organizations. We have firmly established ourselves as a trusted partner in the industry, offering high-quality products and services tailored to meet the specific requirements of each department.

Our unwavering commitment to excellence and customer satisfaction has propelled us to expand our reach and serve numerous government departments. We continue to strive for growth, innovation, and maintaining strong relationships with our valued clients across different sectors.

Govt. departments we serve

1.6 Our Partners

In addition to our extensive work with government organizations, we have fostered robust partnerships with industry giants and renowned companies. Some of the notable industry players we have been serving include:

1. L&T (Larsen & Toubro)

2. Shapoorji Pallonji

3. BG Shirke

4. Parnika Builders

5. DLF (Delhi Land & Finance)

6. JP Builders

7. Dilip Buildcon

8. Punj Lloyd

These examples represent just a fraction of the prominent companies we have had the privilege to serve over the years. Our commitment to delivering high-quality products, innovative solutions, and excellent customer service has been instrumental in cultivating long-term relationships with industry leaders.

We take great pride in our ability to cater to the diverse needs and requirements of both government organizations and private sector giants. Our extensive expertise and reliable services have made us a trusted partner for these industry giants, contributing to their successful projects and operations.

As we continue to expand our reach and strengthen our partnerships, we remain dedicated to providing exceptional services and contributing to the growth and success of our esteemed clients.

Chapter 2

The Real Why:
Behind why I wrote This Book

After interviewing many top government officials like Garrison Engineers, Executive Engineers and prominent private builders and project managers, I have identified several challenges commonly faced by government officials, engineers, and project managers in the infrastructure industry. These challenges can significantly impact the smooth execution of projects. Let's address each challenge one by one:

Certainly, addressing these challenges is crucial for the successful execution of infrastructure projects. Now, let's delve into each challenge and explore potential solutions:

Challenge 1

Is the supplied product at your project site genuine or fake?

To ensure product authenticity, it is essential to establish strong partnerships with trusted suppliers. Conduct thorough due diligence, verify certifications, and perform quality checks on received products to mitigate the risk of counterfeit or fake items.

Challenge 2

Difficulty in choosing the right product that best suits your demand?

To address this challenge, it is crucial to perform a comprehensive needs assessment. Engage in thorough research to understand the project requirements, considering factors such as durability, performance, and compliance with industry standards. Seek expert advice, consult with industry professionals, and evaluate product specifications and performance to make informed decisions aligned with your specific needs.

Challenge 3

Are you stuck whether the supplied products are meeting the required specifications?

Establish clear communication channels with suppliers. Clearly define and communicate the specific quality standards and specifications for the required products.. Implement robust quality control measures, including regular inspections and testing, to ensure the received products meet the required specifications.

Challenge 4

World is growing at a lightning speed in terms of innovation, are we using innovative products for ourselves?

To stay ahead in the industry, it is essential to stay updated with the latest trends, innovations, and technological advancements. Engage in research and development activities to explore and evaluate innovative products and solutions. Attend industry conferences, workshops, and seminars to gain insights and network with innovative companies. Foster partnerships and collaborations with technology-driven organizations to adopt cutting-edge products and solutions that can enhance project efficiency and effectiveness.

Challenge 5

Are you sure that you are using 100% hygienic products?

Ensure compliance with hygiene and safety regulations specific to your industry. Collaborate with suppliers who prioritize product hygiene and quality control. Implement rigorous hygiene protocols, conduct regular inspections, and maintain detailed documentation to ensure compliance with hygiene standards.

Challenge 6

Do you need to replace your products frequently?

Choose high-quality, durable products from reputable suppliers to reduce the need for frequent replacements. Prioritize longevity and reliability when making purchasing decisions. Conduct proper maintenance and inspections to extend the lifespan of products.

Challenge 7

Are your infra projects stealing your peace of mind?

Implement effective project management strategies, including proper planning, risk assessment, and transparent communication with stakeholders. Foster a collaborative work environment, empower your team, and leverage project management tools and methodologies to proactively identify and address challenges, ensuring smoother project execution and peace of mind.

Challenge 8

Do you know how to complete a project on the first attempt with 100% success?

Invest in thorough project planning, including detailed feasibility studies, risk analysis, and contingency planning. Utilize experienced professionals, adopt robust project management methodologies, and foster effective communication and collaboration among team members and stakeholders to increase the chances of project success on the first attempt.

Challenge 9

Even after buying the best products, not getting desired results?

Ensure proper product installation, follow manufacturer guidelines, and conduct performance testing. If the desired results are not achieved, identify potential issues and consult with experts or suppliers to troubleshoot and rectify the problem.

Challenge 10

Do you have to extend project timelines?

Implement realistic project planning, accounting for potential delays and unforeseen circumstances. Regularly monitor project progress, identify bottlenecks early, and take proactive measures to mitigate delays. Effective communication and coordination among stakeholders are essential for timely project completion. Evaluate project timelines periodically and adjust as necessary to ensure realistic and achievable milestones.

Challenge 11

Are you still using old-age products or innovative ones?

Stay updated with the latest industry advancements and product innovations. Evaluate the benefits of adopting new technologies and products that align with your project requirements. Collaborate with suppliers, and industry experts, and research organizations to explore innovative solutions that can enhance project outcomes and improve efficiency.

Challenge 12

Are you relying only on paperwork or using a framework to check product quality and specifications?

Implement a robust quality assurance framework that includes physical inspections, testing, and documentation. Combine on-site inspections with paperwork and leverage digital tools for streamlined data management and analysis. Establish clear criteria and standards for product quality and specifications. Engage in regular audits and assessments to ensure compliance with quality standards.

Challenge 13

Do you know how you can save crores of government funds?

Implement cost optimization strategies such as conducting thorough cost analysis, value engineering, and exploring alternative materials or technologies. Foster transparent procurement processes, encourage competitive bidding, and engage in negotiations to secure cost-effective deals. Embrace efficient project management practices to minimize delays and cost overruns. Regularly monitor and track project expenses to identify potential cost-saving opportunities. Collaborate with finance and procurement teams to streamline budget allocation and utilization.

By addressing these challenges with proactive measures and implementing best practices, you can enhance project outcomes and achieve success in your infrastructure projects.

Chapter 3

THE BIG PROMISE

There is one thing that I want to assure you, which I call my "BIG PROMISE." After reading and implementing the guidance and strategies provided in this book, you will be able to achieve the following outcomes on your own, guaranteed:

1. Successfully complete projects with greater profitability, prestige, peace of mind, and timely completion.

2. Bring innovation to your project to become a "TORCHBEARER," leading positive change in your department.

3. Avoid falling victim to duplicity and ensure the use of genuine and authentic products in your projects.

4. Protect yourself and your team from being identified for negligence or improper project execution, fostering a culture of accountability and professionalism.

The author's commitment to helping readers achieve these outcomes demonstrates their confidence in the effectiveness of the book's content. By sharing insights, experiences, and practical advice, the author aims to equip readers with the necessary tools to overcome challenges and excel in their project management endeavors.

Chapter 4

Counterfeiting A Menace

After conducting extensive research for this book, I came across an interesting study titled "Counterfeit Brands, Consumer Attitude, And Initiatives To Stop Counterfeiting In India," published by Global Journals Inc. (USA).

The study says "The intention of consumers to buy counterfeit products can be influenced by various factors.

4.1 Consumer behavior

Here are six key factors that can impact consumers' inclination towards purchasing counterfeit items."

1. **Social Dimension:** Social factors play a significant role in consumers' intention to buy counterfeit products. This includes influences from friends, family, and social circles, as well as the desire to fit in or be accepted by a particular group.

2. **Personal Gratification:** Consumers may be driven by the personal gratification they derive from owning counterfeit products. This can be associated withthe perceived status, prestige, or satisfaction they believe these products provide, regardless of their authenticity.

3. **Perception:** Consumers' perception of counterfeit products and their quality can influence their intention to purchase them. If consumers believe that the counterfeit products closely resemble the genuine ones in terms of appearance, functionality, or performance, they may be more inclined to buy them.

4. **Value:** The perception of value for money is another important factor. Consumers may view counterfeit products as cheaper alternatives to genuine ones, and if they believe they can obtain similar benefits or utility at a lower cost, they may opt for counterfeit goods.

5. **Ethics:** Consumers' ethical considerations and moral judgments can impact their intention to buy counterfeit products. Some consumers reject counterfeit products due to concerns related to intellectual property rights infringement, supporting illegal activities, or contributing to the loss of revenue for legitimate businesses.

6. **Brand Loyalty:** Consumers' loyalty to a specific brand can influence their decision to buy counterfeit products. If consumers have lower loyalty to a particular brand or perceive high prices associated with genuine products, they may be more open to considering counterfeit alternatives.

These factors are not exhaustive, and individual consumer attitudes and behaviors can vary. It is important to note that promoting and purchasing counterfeit products is illegal and can have negative consequences for both consumers and businesses.

Another survey conducted by Global Journals Inc. (USA) examines "how the price factor can influence consumer behavior."

"The survey respondents were evenly distributed between the Indian and American markets. Based on the results, it was found that respondents from India were more price-conscious and more inclined to purchasing counterfeits."

4.2 The price factor

The price factor is a significant influence on consumer behavior and can have a profound impact on their purchasing decisions. Here are the 5 ways in which price can alter consumer behavior:

1. **Perception of Value:** Consumers frequently evaluate the worth of a product based on its price. A higher price is often associated with superior quality, prestige, or exclusivity, leading consumers to perceive the product as more valuable. Conversely, a lower price may be seen as an indicator of lower quality or inferiority influencing consumers to perceive the product as less valuable..

2. **Price Sensitivity:** Consumers differ in their sensitivity to price changes. Some consumers are highly price-sensitive and actively seek out lower-priced options, while others are less price-sensitive and may prioritize other factors such as quality or brand reputation. Understanding the price sensitivity of target consumers can help businesses set appropriate pricing strategies.

3. **Price-Quality Relationship:** Consumers often perceive a relationship between price and quality. Higher-priced

products are often assumed to be of higher quality, while lower-priced products may be seen as lower in quality. This perception can significantly impact consumer behavior, as individuals may be willing to pay more for products they believe are of higher quality.

4. **Price as an Indicator of Value:** Consumers often rely on price as a heuristic or shortcut to evaluate the value of a product. They may assume that a higher-price corresponds to better features, benefits, or performance compared to lower-priced alternatives. Price serves as a signal or cue that shapes consumer perceptions and decision-making.

5. **Price as a Competitive Advantage:** In competitive markets, businesses can leverage pricing strategies to attract consumers and gain a competitive edge. Lowering prices can stimulate demand, attract price-sensitive consumers, or encourage trial purchases. Price adjustments, discounts, or promotions can influence consumer behavior by creating a sense of urgency or perceived value.

It's important to note that the impact of price on consumer behavior can vary across different industries, products, and target markets.

4.3 Impact of counterfeiting on global and Indian economy

Counterfeit and pirated products have indeed emerged as a significant global challenge, exerting substantial economic consequences. The estimated value of counterfeit and pirated products may vary across different reports and studies. Nonetheless, it is crucial to recognize that counterfeiting and piracy pose significant economic hurdles.

According to a report published by the Organization for Economic Co-operation and Development (OECD) and the European Union Intellectual Property Office (EUIPO), the global trade in counterfeit and pirated goods was estimated to be worth approximately $509 billion in 2016. However, it is important to note that this figure only accounts for physical goods and does not encompass the full scope of the issue, including digital piracy and other forms of counterfeiting.

A report commissioned by the International Trademark Association (INTA) and the International Chamber of Commerce, projects that the global economic value of counterfeiting and piracy could reach $2.3 trillion by 2022. Today in 2023, these projected figures have surpassed beyond our wildest imagination), taking over 5% of the global GDP. This staggering figure highlights the significant economic implications posed by counterfeiting and piracy.

Counterfeiting and piracy pose significant economic challenges, including lost revenues for legitimate businesses, job losses, hindrance to innovation, compromised consumer safety, and the funding of illicit activities. To effectively address these challenges, collaborative efforts from governments, businesses, and consumers are required. This includes enforcing intellectual property rights, raising awareness about the issue, implementing stricter regulations, and promoting ethical consumption practices.

It's important to stay informed about the issue and support initiatives aimed at combating counterfeiting and piracy to safeguard industries, economies, and consumers from the detrimental effects of these illicit activities.

4.4 What is counterfeiting and why it occurs

Counterfeiting refers to the unauthorized production, distribution, or sale of goods that imitate or replicate genuine products. without proper authorization or licensing from the rightful owners. These counterfeit products are designed to deceive consumers by closely imitating the appearance, packaging, trademarks, and overall branding of genuine products. However, it is important to note that counterfeit goods are typically of inferior quality and may pose significant risks to consumers, as they do not undergo the same rigorous quality measures and safety regulations as genuine products.

Counterfeiting occurs due to a variety of reasons, driven by economic, social, and technological factors. Here are some key reasons why counterfeiting happens:

1. **Profit Motive:** Counterfeiters are driven by the desire to generate illicit profits by selling counterfeit goods at lower prices compared to genuine products. They exploit consumer demand for popular brands and take advantage of price differentials to attract buyers.

2. **Lack of Legal Consequences:** In many cases, the penalties for counterfeiting are not stringent enough to effectively deter counterfeiters. Weak enforcement of intellectual

property laws and limited resources for investigations and prosecutions contribute to the persistence of counterfeiting activities.

3. **Globalization and Supply Chains:** The globalization of trade and complex supply chains have facilitated the infiltration of counterfeiters into legitimate distribution channels. Counterfeit products can be manufactured in one country, distributed through multiple intermediaries, and sold in another, making it challenging to trace the origin and disrupt the supply chain.

4. **Advancements in Technology:** Technological advancements have made it easier for counterfeiters to produce convincing replicas of genuine products. Sophisticated printing techniques, online marketplaces, and digital platforms provide counterfeiters with the tools and platforms they need to advertise, sell, and distribute their counterfeit goods.

5. **Consumer Demand and Affordability:** Consumers seeking popular brands at lower prices may unknowingly contribute to the demand for counterfeit products. The allure of purchasing luxury items or well-known brands at discounted rates can lead some consumers to buy counterfeit goods, often unaware of the risks associated with such products.

6. **Lack of Awareness:** Insufficient consumer awareness about the risks and consequences of buying counterfeit products can contribute to the perpetuation of counterfeiting.

Educating consumers about the potential dangers, including health risks, compromised quality, and support for illicit activities, can help combat counterfeiting.

Addressing counterfeiting requires a comprehensive approach that engages governments, law enforcement agencies, intellectual property rights holders, businesses, and consumers. It is crucial to strengthen intellectual property laws, enhance enforcement efforts, raising awareness, promote ethical consumption, and implement rigorous supply chain management practices. These measures are vital in combating counterfeiting and safeguarding the interests of consumers and legitimate businesses.

In a nutshell counterfeit brands are fake or unauthorized copy of the genuine brands.

Counterfeit brands are produced with the intention of exploiting the brand image of genuine brands. Manufacturer copies the logo and uses it to sell counterfeit products in the market. Unfortunately, counterfeit products sometimes become the reason for the death of thousands of people.

4.5 Classification of counterfeiting- Two major types

Deceptive -When a consumer is not aware

Deceptive counterfeit brands are sold in the market with the intention to fool the customer and make them believe that they are purchasing an authorized brand. This deceptive practice takes advantage of consumers' lack of awareness.

Non-Deceptive- In which consumer distinguishes that the product on the basis of its genuineness through information given on the packets, price, sales area and the substances used to produce the counterfeit products. and then takes the decision to purchase- But "All this information is False, and designed to deceive the customer."

4.6 Counterfeiting – is an evil and it's spread beyond economy

Counterfeit products lack warranty and introduce financial risks for consumers. Factors such as awareness, greed and social influence can influence consumers' attitude towards counterfeit brands.

Undoubtedly, counterfeiting poses significant challenges and risks to communities, economies, and legal systems. Here are some key points highlighting the severity of counterfeiting:

1. **Economic Impact:** Counterfeiting has a detrimental impact on the economy of a country. It leads to revenue losses for legitimate businesses, job losses, and reduced investments. Counterfeit goods undermine the competitiveness of genuine products, affecting industries and hindering economic growth.

2. **Consumer Safety and Health Risks:** Counterfeit products often do not undergo the same quality control measures and safety regulations as genuine products. This poses significant risks to consumers' safety and health. For example, counterfeit pharmaceuticals can contain harmful

ingredients or incorrect dosages, jeopardizing the well-being of individuals.

3. **Legal System Challenges:** Counterfeiting poses significant challenges for legal system as it requires allocating resources to enforce intellectual property rights, conduct investigations, and initiate legal proceedings against counterfeiters. The complexity of global supply chains and the involvement of organized crime networks further complicate the efforts to combat counterfeiting.

4. **Brand Reputation and Consumer Trust:** Counterfeit products undermine the reputation and trust of genuine brands. When consumers unknowingly purchase counterfeit goods that do not meet quality standards, it can create a negative perception of the brand. This loss of customer trust can result in a decline in customer loyalty and potential revenue loss for the brand.

5. **Lost Tax Revenues:** Counterfeit trade leads to substantial losses in tax revenue losses for governments. Since counterfeit goods are frequently sold in the informal market or through illicit channels, the government loses out on tax revenues that could have been generated from legitimate sales.

6. **Funding Illicit Activities:** Counterfeit trade is commonly associated with organized crime networks and illicit activities, including money laundering, drug trafficking, and terrorism financing. The profits derived from counterfeiting can provide financial support for criminal operations, thereby undermining societal well-being and security.

Addressing counterfeiting requires a multi-faceted approach that includes robust legal frameworks, effective enforcement measures, public awareness campaigns, and collaboration among government agencies, law enforcement, businesses, and consumers. By raising awareness about the risks associated with counterfeit products and promoting ethical consumption, we can reduce the demand for counterfeit goods and protect the interests of both consumers and legitimate businesses.

4.7 India is one of the largest markets for counterfeit brands.

Resulting in significant losses to the Indian economy and Industries amounting to billions and trillions rupees. Counterfeit products also pose risks to millions of individual consumers in terms of health and safety.

The report titled 'Illicit markets: A threat to National Interests' says that India's illicit market, spread across five key industries, has cost India 3 million jobs. The government has suffered a 58521 crore loss due to the counterfeit market in 2019-2020, said the report which was released by former Vice President of India, Venkaiah Naidu.

As per a report published in the Economic Times in 2019, the Authentication Solution Providers' Association (ASPA), consisting of 60 members, mainly focuses on the adoption and advancement of authentication technology and solutions to protect brands, revenue, and documents. Counterfeiting in India has resulted in losses of around Rs 1.05 lakh crore annually, and these figures are expected to nearly double by the end of 2023. The organization for Economic Co-operation and Development (OECD) states that every 4th product sold in India is a counterfeited one, with the maximum impact seen in shoes, clothing, watches and electrical equipment.

The estimated revenue losses for the Indian government due to the counterfeit market are approximately 2 lakh crore INR. It is important to note that the actual industry losses are often much higher than the government losses. Here is an estimated breakdown of the losses in various industries:

1. **Plastic Industry:** The plastic industry incurs losses of around 1000 crores INR due to counterfeiting activities.

2. **Pharmaceutical Industry:** The drug industry suffers losses of approximately 2000 crores INR due to counterfeit drugs entering the market.

3. **Film Industry:** The film industry in India experiences losses of around 2700 crores INR due to piracy and the distribution of counterfeit DVDs and digital content.

4. **Book Publishers:** The publishing industry faces losses of approximately 380 crores INR due to counterfeiting of books and unauthorized reproduction.

5. **Software Industry:** The software industry incurs losses of around 2900 crores INR due to the use and distribution of pirated software.

6. **Automobile Industry:** The automobile industry suffers losses of approximately 1500 crores INR due to the production and sale of counterfeit automobile parts.

These figures highlight the significant financial impact of counterfeiting on various sectors in India. Counterfeit products not only harm legitimate businesses and industries but also contribute to revenue losses for the government. It is imperative to Implement more robust enforcement measures, raising awareness, and promoting the use of genuine products are crucial steps in addressing this issue and reducing the associated losses.

4.8 The initiatives to curb the menace

Indeed, the Indian government, in collaboration with non-governmental organizations, has undertaken numerous initiatives to combat counterfeiting and raise awareness among citizens. These initiatives aim to establish a robust legal framework and educate consumers about the dangers associated with counterfeit products. Here are some notable government initiatives in India:

1. **Intellectual Property Rights (IPR) Protection:** The government has strengthened the legal framework for intellectual property rights protection. Laws and regulations, such as the Trademarks Act, Copyright Act, and Design Act, offer legal remedies for businesses to protect their intellectual property rights.

2. **Enforcement Agencies:** Specialized enforcement agencies such as the Central Bureau of Investigation (CBI), Directorate of Revenue Intelligence (DRI), and Economic Offences Wing (EOW), are dedicated to identifying and prosecuting counterfeiters. These agencies conduct raids and investigations to seize counterfeit products and apprehend individuals involved in counterfeiting activities.

3. **Anti-Counterfeiting Campaigns:** The government, in collaboration with industry associations and non-governmental organizations, conducts awareness campaigns to educate consumers about the risks associated with counterfeit products. These campaigns aim to alter consumer behavior and promote the use of genuine products.

4. **Technology Adoption:** The government encourages the adoption of technological solutions to combat counterfeiting. Measures such as barcode labeling, holograms, RFID (Radio-Frequency Identification), and track-and-trace systems are implemented to enhance product authentication and traceability.

5. **Collaboration with Industry:** The government collaborates with industry stakeholders, including manufacturers, brand owners, and trade associations, to develop strategies and exchange intelligence for effective counterfeiting prevention. Joint initiatives are undertaken to raise awareness, share best practices, and strengthen supply chain security.

6. **International Cooperation:** The Indian government actively engages in international forums and collaborations to address counterfeiting on a global scale. By cooperating with international organizations and other countries, valuable information, intelligence, and best practices are shared to effectively tackle cross-border counterfeiting activities.

These initiatives, taken together, aim to create a strong deterrent against counterfeiting, protect consumers' interests, safeguard legitimate businesses, and ensure a safe and fair marketplace. Through the implementation of comprehensive measures, the Indian government strives to control counterfeiting and mitigate its impact on the economy and society.

Campaigns aimed at controlling counterfeiting play a crucial role in raising awareness and educating consumers about the risks and consequences associated with purchasing counterfeit products. Here are some notable campaigns in India:

1. **"Jaago Grahak Jaago" (Wake up, Consumer, Wake up):** This campaign, initiated by the Ministry of Consumer Affairs, aims to empower consumers by spreading awareness about their rights and responsibilities. It encourages consumers to make informed choices and avoid purchasing counterfeit and substandard products.

2. **"Bhagidari" (Partnership):** This campaign focuses on building partnerships between the government, industry, and consumers to tackle counterfeiting. It emphasizes the role of each stakeholder in creating a counterfeit-free ecosystem.

3. **"Hum Kishore Festival" (We Are Youth Festival):** This initiative targets the youth and educates them about the risks associated with purchasing counterfeit products. It aims to promote responsible consumption and discourage the demand for counterfeit goods.

4. **"Fight Smuggling and Counterfeiting"**: This campaign, led by enforcement agencies such as the Directorate of Revenue Intelligence (DRI) and the Central Board of Indirect Taxes and Customs (CBIC), focuses on combating smuggling and counterfeiting activities. It includes awareness programs, seminars, and workshops aimed at educating the public about the economic and social impact of counterfeiting.

In addition to campaigns, India has implemented a strong legal framework to control counterfeiting. Some key legislations include:

1. **The Drugs and Cosmetics Act, 1940:** This act regulates the manufacturing, sale, and distribution of drugs and cosmetics in India, ensuring their safety, efficacy, and quality.

2. **The Copyright Act, 1957:** This act provides protection to original literary, artistic, and musical works, including software, against unauthorized reproduction and distribution.

3. **The Patents Act, 1970:** This act grants exclusive rights to inventors for their inventions and prohibits the production and sale of counterfeit patented products.

4. **The Trademarks Act, 1999:** This act protects registered trademarks and prohibits the unauthorized use of identical or similar marks that may cause confusion among consumers.

5. **The Designs Act, 2000:** This act provides protection to the visual aspects of industrial designs, preventing their unauthorized reproduction or imitation.

6. **The IT Act, 2000:** This act addresses various cybercrimes, including online counterfeiting and intellectual property infringements.

7. **The Food Safety and Standards Act, 2006:** This act ensures the safety and quality of food products and prohibits the sale of counterfeit or adulterated food items.

These legal frameworks play a crucial role in deterring counterfeiting activities and providing legal remedies for intellectual property rights owners and consumers.

4.9 The conclusion

In conclusion, counterfeiting is a pervasive global problem that presents a significant threat to the global economy and can have harmful and dangerous consequences for people's lives. However, by fostering a combined effort between authorized brand manufacturers and government officials, the sale of counterfeit and fake brands can be effectively stopped. By implementing stronger enforcement measures, raising awareness among consumers, and promoting ethical consumption practices, we can protect consumers, safeguard legitimate businesses, and mitigate the impact of counterfeiting.

Chapter 5

Authenticity

Lets understand Authenticity with this picture

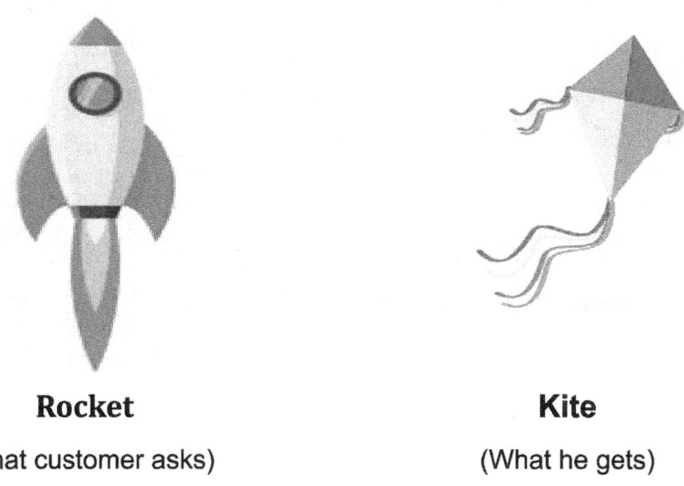

Rocket

(What customer asks)

Kite

(What he gets)

Authenticity is a crucial aspect when it comes to customer expectations and delivering the actual product they desire. To illustrate this concept, let's draw a comparison between a rocket and a kite:

Customer Expectation: When a customer expresses their desire for a rocket, they hold certain expectations in mind. They envision a powerful and high-speed flying capable of soaring through the sky, reaching great heights and covering substantial distances.

What They Get: However, if instead of receiving a rocket, they are given a kite, their expectations remain unfulfilled. A kite is a completely different object that operates differently. It is a lightweight object that requires wind to fly and is controlled by a string attached to it.

In this analogy, the rocket symbolizes the genuine and authentic product that perfectly matches the customer's expectations. It aligns with their desires and effectively serves its intended purpose. On the other hand, the kite represents a counterfeit or inferior product that fails to meet the customer's expectations and may not deliver the desired experience.

Authenticity is crucial because customers rely on it to make informed decisions and trust that the product they receive will deliver the desired benefits and meet their needs. When authenticity is compromised, it can lead to disappointment, mistrust, and negative experiences for the customer.

Therefore, it becomes imperative for businesses and manufacturers to prioritize the authenticity of their products, ensuring that customers receive exactly what they seek and that promises are fulfilled. This builds trust, strengthens customer relationships, and enhances overall satisfaction.

Fake products: Poor Quality

So there is a need to repeatedly replace the products, resulting in significant costs amounting to crores of government funds.

5.1 The Financial Burden

Indeed, the presence of fake products with poor quality can result in significant financial losses, especially for government-funded projects. The need to repeatedly replace these substandard products can lead to substantial expenses, ultimately costing the government crores of rupees. This financial burden arises due to several factors:

1. **Product Failure:** Counterfeit products are more prone to failure, malfunction, or premature wear and tear. They may not meet the required specifications or industry standards, resulting in frequent breakdowns and the need for replacements. Each replacement incurs additional costs in terms of procurement, installation, and labor.

2. **Increased Maintenance and Repair Expenses:** Poor-quality counterfeit products often require more frequent maintenance and repairs. These ongoing expenses can quickly accumulate, putting strain on the project budget and diverting funds from other critical aspects.

3. **Delayed Project Timelines:** When counterfeit products fail or require replacement, it can cause project delays. These delays further impact the overall project schedule, prolonging the time required for completion. The extended project timelines result in additional costs, such as extended labor and administrative expenses.

4. **Inefficiencies and Productivity Losses:** Counterfeit products contribute to inefficiencies and productivity losses within a project. When these products fail to meet expectations or perform as required, they disrupt the smooth operation of the project, resulting in wasted time, effort, and resources. This inefficiency can impact the overall productivity and effectiveness of the project, leading to financial losses.

5.2 Victims of counterfeiting and inauthenticity

I'm sorry to hear about Lt. Col. V.K. Pandey's 2005 case (referenced from India Kanoon website), where he fought his case for 15 years but he could not get his promotion even after. Currently, there are approximately 3000 pending cases against GEs, CEs, EEs, CWEs, their teams, or vendors, involving allegations of negligence and improper project execution. In 2022 alone, there were about 400 cases, and unfortunately, these numbers continue to rise each year.

Cases involving negligence and authenticity can have serious consequences and can impact the professional growth and reputation of individuals involved. It is crucial for organizations and authorities to address these cases promptly and fairly, ensuring justice and accountability are upheld.

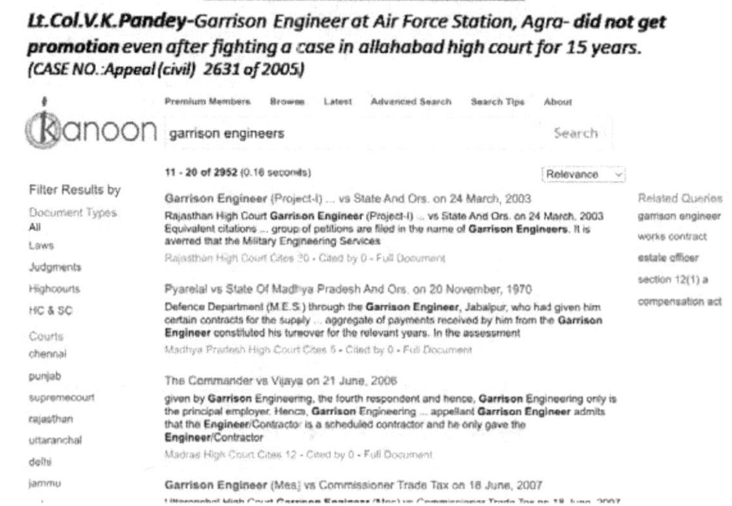

5.3 Adhering to quality, originality and authenticity

We take pride in our extensive manufacturing capabilities, offering a diverse selection of water tanks with various capacities and designs. Our products are meticulously crafted in accordance with the IS 12701 and ISO specifications, underscoring our unwavering commitment to quality and compliance. Additionally, we have taken the initiative to register our brands with both major and minor government and private departments, further exemplifying our dedication to serving a wide range of clients.

The registration of renowned brands such as TUFF, DHARA, ROTEX, UNIPLAST, UNITANK, and ROTOPLAST exclusively with esteemed organizations like MES and CPWD showcases our recognition and acceptance in the industry. It highlights our ability to meet the requirements and standards set by these prestigious departments.

By offering a diverse range of water tanks and registering our brands, we ensure that customers have access to dependable and trustworthy solutions for their water storage needs. This contributes to our credibility and strengthens our position in the market.

We strive to Keep up the good work in providing high-quality water tanks and serving various government and private departments with your registered brands.

Water Tanks as per is 12701:1996: Approved in all Govt. Departments

5.4 The Solution

After discussing the various aspects related to counterfeiting and authenticity, it becomes evident that you have identified the major challenges you face in this regard. Two key questions emerge:1. How to identify whether a product is genuine or fake? 2. How to know whether a product meets the required specifications?

Upon careful consideration and deeper analysis, you will find that almost 80% of the problems can be traced back to these two fundamental issues. Whether it is the delay in project execution, project cost increase, negligence, frequent replacement of supplies products and or the mental agony experienced when things do not go as planned, the root cause often lies in the authenticity and adherence to specifications of the products involved.

Here is the solution of all these problems

Identifying whether a product is genuine or fake and ensuring that it meets the required specifications are indeed crucial challenges when it comes to counterfeiting and authenticity. To address this, consider the following:

1. **Authenticity verification:** Look for key indicators of authenticity such as holograms, serial numbers, or unique markings on the product or its packaging. Cross-check these indicators with official records or authentication databases provided by the manufacturer or relevant authorities.

2. **Authorized distribution channels:** To avoid counterfeit products, only purchase products from authorized sellers,

distributors, or retailers who have a legitimate partnership or affiliation with the brand. Be cautious of unauthorized sellers or suspicious online platforms known for selling counterfeit products.

3. **Quality assurance:** Familiarize yourself with the genuine product's packaging, labeling, and overall quality. Pay attention to any discrepancies or signs of poor craftsmanship, such as misspellings, low-quality materials, or inferior printing. Consider comparing the product with trusted sources or consulting experts who can provide insights into its genuine characteristics.

4. **Certification and documentation:** Look for certifications, test reports, or quality assurance documents that accompany the product. Genuine products often come with proper documentation that validates their authenticity and compliance with industry standards.

5. **Manufacturer's website or official channels:** Visit the manufacturer's official website or contact their customer support to verify the authenticity of the product. They may provide specific guidelines or tools to help consumers authenticate their products.

6. **Seek professional assistance:** If you have suspicions or concerns regarding a product's authenticity, seek professional assistance from brand representatives, industry experts, or third-party authentication services. These professionals can offer expertise and guidance in determining the product's authenticity and adherence to specifications.

5.5 In summary

To mitigate these issues and reduce the financial burden caused by fake products, it is crucial to enforce strict quality control measures, promote awareness among consumers and procurement agencies, and support reliable and authorized suppliers. By ensuring the authenticity and quality of products used in government projects, the need for frequent replacements can be minimized, resulting in substantial cost savings and better utilization of government funds.

Chapter 6

The Innovation

Despite almost two decades having passed, there seems to be a noticeable lack of innovation in water storage technology, as the standards set by the Bureau of Indian Standards (BIS) in 1996 continue to be adhered to. In contrast, we witness innovation in numerous other sectors, including automobiles, mobile devices, computers, housing, appliances, clothing, televisions, and more.

6.1 The problem with the old age conventional water tanks

Water tanks, often located on rooftops, are susceptible to neglect when it comes to maintenance. Many individuals may struggle to recall the last time they inspected their water tank, unless a problem like a burst occurs. The image portrayed highlights the possibility of deterioration and uncleanliness of water tanks, with the potential accumulation of salt, algae, and fungus. While some may argue that they rarely consume water directly from the tank and instead rely on water purification systems like reverse osmosis (RO), it is important to consider water intake during daily activities such as brushing, bathing, and kitchen use.

The presence of such filthy water in tanks can pose significant health risks. Bacteria, viruses, and fungi present in the water can lead to contagious, critical, and even life-threatening diseases,, such as cholera, diarrhea, typhoid, and more, if not promptly addressed. Therefore, it is crucial to address the cleanliness and maintenance of water tanks to mitigate these potential health hazards.

6.2 An interesting true story

I vividly remember a tragic incident that occurred at a prestigious client's site, resulting in the unfortunate loss of a laborer's life due to the consumption of contaminated water. A thorough investigation revealed that the water tanks had been contaminated by a pair of house lizards, specifically the yellow-bellied house Gecko (Hemidactylus flaviviridis). It is crucial to note that these lizards themselves are not poisonous. However, they can harbor harmful bacteria and parasites on their body and skin.

In this particular case, the water temperature played a significant role in the tragic event. The water inside the tanks had reached an approximate temperature 50°C, causing the lizards to decompose. As a result, their bodily fluids, including feces, urine, and other toxins, were released and contaminated the water supply.

The combination of high water temperature and the decomposition process facilitated the mixing of these harmful substances, resulting in the water becoming toxic. The presence of toxins in the water, caused by the interaction between the decomposing lizards and the elevated temperature, had severe health consequences and tragically resulted in the loss of a life.

This incident highlights the critical importance of maintaining proper conditions for water storage, regular inspections, and implementing adequate temperature control measures. It serves as a reminder to ensure that water tanks are securely covered to prevent the entry of contaminants. Furthermore, it is essential to promptly address any potential health hazards related to water storage systems to prevent similar incidents in the future.

A methaphore

Imagine your water tank as a pressure cooker, with the scorching heat of the sun acting like flames. In this metaphor, as the temperature rises above 40°C, an alarming transformation occurs within your water tank. The intense heat acts as a catalyst, causing a chemical reaction between the water and the non-food grade plastic polymers of the tank. This reaction creates a toxic concoction, slowly poisoning the water and posing a significant risk to your health.

6.3 A personal real-life experience of mine

Following the unfortunate incident, let's shift gears and engage in a conversation that combines humor and seriousness. Can you relate to the situation depicted in the picture below? Have you ever found yourself in a similar predicament? Allow me to share an interesting incident of my own. Approximately five years ago, I traveled to Jaipur, Rajasthan with a business colleague to attend a conference. It was the scorching month of May, and fortunately, the temperature hovered around 42-43°C. Thankfully, we avoided visiting in June when temperatures often soared beyond 45-46°C or even higher. In preparation for the conference, we decided to check into a luxurious five-star hotel to freshen up. As we entered the hotel's conference room, my colleague's immediate instinct was to head straight for the restroom. Meanwhile, I settled into a chair in the hotel room, quenching my thirst with a refreshing cold drink and perusing the conference agenda and guest list. Suddenly, I was startled by a cry of distress emanating from the bathroom. Reacting swiftly, I rushed to the bathroom door and inquired anxiously if my colleague was alright. In a state of immense pain, he exclaimed, "Nothing is okay! The scorching water from the bidet has burned my anus, the most sensitive part of the human body!" Suppressing my laughter, I advised him to adjust the bidet's lever to the cold side. To my surprise, he insisted that it was already set to cold. Eventually, we discovered that the actual issue lay with the temperature of the water in the tank. Did you know that the water inside a tank can be substantially hotter than the ambient temperature outside? This phenomenon can be understood by drawing a parallel with the basic concept of a pressure cooker in the kitchen. Just as food cooks faster inside a pressure cooker due to the enclosed environment, where steam and pressure expedite the cooking process, water tanks can experience elevated temperatures due to the accumulation of steam and heat inside. As a result, the water temperature in the tank can surpass the surrounding environment by 5-10°C.

Challenges arising from water temperature fluctuations during summers and winters

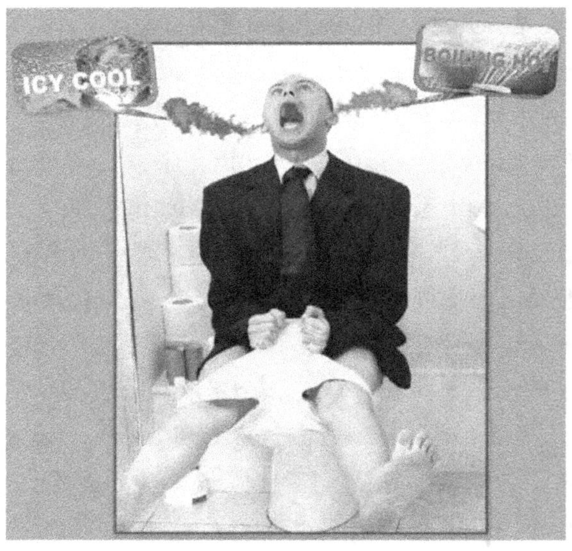

The picture is funny yet true reality

6.4 The Catalyst

This amusing yet significant incident became a catalyst for me to conceive a water storage technology that addresses two critical aspects: the impact of external temperatures ranging from 0*c to 50*c on stored water during both summer and winter seasons, and the need for effectiveness and long-term affordability, unlike traditional steel tanks. Steel tanks, despite their drawbacks, are cumbersome and challenging to handle. Additionally, they are prone to rust caused by water salt and environmental chemical reactions, resulting in unhygienic water. Moreover, steel tanks come with a hefty price tag. Consequently, we embarked on a journey to invent a solution that not only regulates and preserves water temperature but also exhibits durability, hygiene, ease of handling, and long-term cost-effectiveness.

Through a relentless journey filled with challenges and initial setbacks, combined with the utilization of my extensive 17-18 years of experience and expertise, meticulous research, and significant financial investments, we have successfully brought to life an exceptional water storage technology. This technology, now protected by a patent, has the power to free you from all concerns surrounding water storage. Whether it's ensuring precise water temperature control, upholding impeccable hygiene standards, facilitating effortless cleaning and maintenance, guaranteeing food-grade safety, incorporating a modern and sleek design, and much more, this innovative solution covers all aspects. With our groundbreaking water storage technology, you can bid farewell to all your worries, knowing that your water storage needs are comprehensively addressed.

The detrimental impacts of outdated storage technology

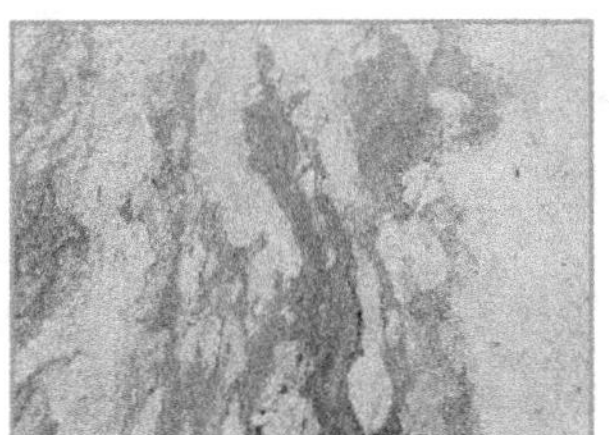

Fungus, algae, lichens, Salt

6.5 The Quick Recap

In summary, we have covered the following key points:

1. The detrimental effects of counterfeiting on health, economy, and job loss.

2. The ability to determine the authenticity of a product without confusion.

3. Resolving any discrepancies between required and supplied goods' specifications.

4. Introduction of an innovative patented modern water storage technology that addresses the current needs.

5. Ensuring successful project completion with improved profitability, peace of mind, and timely delivery.

By addressing these aspects, we can combat counterfeiting, enhance product quality, and achieve better project outcomes.

6.6 Feeling overwhelmed by the multitude of tasks? Don't fret!

I'm here to offer my support. With my assistance, you'll have access to a powerful and customized framework that will enable you to visualize, track, and measure the progress of your project. In addition to the framework, I will provide the necessary training and guidance to ensure your success. You will also have the tools to effectively track resource allocation, manage inventory, and transform your project into a remarkable achievement marked by prestige, profitability, and peace of mind. If you would like further details or would like to avail yourself of my support, please don't hesitate to reach out to me via email at vkaggarwal.hgp@gmail.com or through WhatsApp at +919899580754. As a special offer, the first 100 inquiries will receive my support entirely free of charge.

Please note that I may experience delays in responding due to my busy schedule, but rest assured, you will receive a response from me.

NOTES: ✍

NOTES:

NOTES:

www.ingramcontent.com/pod-product-compliance
Lightning Source LLC
LaVergne TN
LVHW051311200726
843510LV00010B/1366